OUR Pieceful Village

LYNN RICE

That Patchwork Place ®

MISSION STATEMENT

WE ARE DEDICATED TO PROVIDING QUALITY PRODUCTS THAT ENCOURAGE CREATIVITY AND PROMOTE SELF-ESTEEM IN OUR CUSTOMERS AND OUR EMPLOYEES.

WE STRIVE TO MAKE A DIFFERENCE IN THE LIVES WE TOUCH.

That Patchwork Place is an employee-owned, financially secure company.

Our Pieceful Village ©
© 1994 by Lynn Rice
That Patchwork Place, Inc.,
PO Box 118, Bothell, WA 98041-0118 USA

Printed in The United States of America
99 98 97 96 95 94   6 5 4 3 2 1

Library of Congress Cataloging-in-Publication Data

Rice, Lynn,
    Our pieceful village / Lynn Rice.
      p.   cm.
    ISBN 1-56477-071-0 :
    1. Patchwork—Patterns. 2. Quilting—Patterns. 3. Cities and towns in art. I. Title.
TT835.R53 1994
746.46—dc20   94-18421
                           CIP

Acknowledgments

My sincere thanks go to:

Sharon, for her encouragement and support;

Cheryl, Colleen, Ellen, Ginger, Jane, Joyce, Lesley, Lindsay, Melinda, Myra, Susan, and Suzy, whose enthusiasm kept me going;

My sister Millie, for helping me be "the best of whatever I am" and for her wonderful hand-dyed fabrics;

All my customers, whose creative skills in taking a simple design and making beautiful quilts surpassed my wildest expectations;

And lastly, the wonderful husbands who helped in many ways, especially in hanging the quilt show.

Dedication

To my family.
To Art for being my best friend.
To Andrew, Sarah, and Daniel
for their love.

Credits

Editor-in-Chief .... Barbara Weiland
Technical Editors .... Janet White
                                      Sharon Rose
Managing Editor .... Greg Sharp
Copy Editor .... Tina Cook
Proofreader .... Leslie Phillips
Design Director .... Judy Petry
Typesetter .... Typesetter Plus
Photographer .... Brent Kane
Illustrator .... Typesetter Plus

CONTENTS

Introduction 4
General Directions 5
   Fabric Selection 5
   Tools 6
   Getting Organized 6
The Blocks... 7
   Cape Cod Cottage 7
   Farmhouse 10
   Barn 13
   Apple Tree and Clothesline 17
   Grove of Trees 20
   Lake 23
   Gazebo 34
   Quilt Shop 37
   Signs and Fence 40
   Church... 43
   Log Cabin 47
   School 50
Finishing... 54
Sources for Supplies 55
Miniature Conversion Chart................... 56
Meet the Author 56

Gallery 25

INTRODUCTION

This book grew out of a quiltmaking class I teach at my quilt shop, A Touch of Amish, ltd., in Barrington, Illinois. Sampler quilts are wonderful teaching tools because each block incorporates different techniques, and together they make one quilt. Because my staff and I feel so strongly about the teaching value of sampler quilts, we have based our Block of the Month program on a sampler quilt each year.

Having taught samplers with a variety of settings, we needed something different, something that would keep the attention of the students who had been coming to us through the years. I created "Our Pieceful Village" out of this desire for a brand new, unique sampler quilt. It is simple enough that a beginner can manage the techniques, but open-ended enough to intrigue the most experienced quilter.

The response to "Our Pieceful Village" was wonderful. Students far surpassed our expectations. They were creative in their use of fabrics and developed skills with an enthusiasm we had not seen before. They added appliqué and pieced "extras" all over their quilts. Their quilts told stories and depicted seasons and holidays, from Halloween to Christmas to a summer vacation.

Whether you make the quilt on your own or as part of a class, I hope you will let your imagination run wild just as my students did!

There once was a patchwork quilt
Made of houses so carefully built.
Pieced of stripes, plaids, and print
Of all colors, shades, and tint.

There are houses, barn, and a church
With a lake for sailing and perch.
There is a fence, gazebo, and school
Now follow the road to discover the rule:
All the roads will lead you one way
To the quilt shop without further delay.

For now is the time to choose
The colors and fabrics you'll use.
Choose a season and time of day.
Will there be sun or clouds of gray?
Will the grass be gold or green?
Perhaps covered with snow so clean.

The houses you'll cut, trim, and sew
From houses to homes they will grow.
With your care, thoughts, and touch
Your "pieceful village" will mean so much.

You will measure, iron, and snip.
Also quilt, bind, and hopefully, not rip,
To produce your very own patchwork quilt
Made of houses so carefully built.

Lynn Rice

GENERAL DIRECTIONS

This quilt is fun to create. It is simple and clear enough for the beginner, but entertaining enough for the more experienced. You will use fabric to create architectural details and add your own unique touches. Piecing is done with short-cuts, or "tricks," and is Template-Free®.

Don't forget to press the seams of your block as you construct it. Generally, you will press seams toward the darker fabric. Watch for opportunities to create subtle dimensional effects with your pressing. Pressing seams away from a shape can cause that shape to recede visually.

Note: A special feature of this quilt is the "cutting cushion." Even though you use a ¼"-wide seam allowance to piece the blocks, no matter how carefully you piece, variations in size will occur. Every block in this book has extra fabric added along two sides to compensate for this. The directions for each block include instructions for trimming the pieced block to its proper dimensions. Follow these directions carefully and your blocks will fit together in the end. The finished quilt measures approximately 67" x 70".

FABRIC SELECTION

First, choose a color scheme for the finished quilt—a season, a time of day, or even weather conditions. It could be the Fourth of July or Christmas Eve. The sky and the windows can be light or dark. Your options are endless.

Do not purchase all of your fabrics at one time. I used about thirty different fabrics in my quilt—too many decisions to make at once. (To be honest, you don't need that many different fabrics. You could repeat more than I did, but I was having fun.)

Choose your background, sky, and walkway. Pick out a few fabrics for building sidings, roofs, and windows, and add more as you go along.

Dealing with fabrics efficiently requires some planning. Whenever possible, cut long crosswise-grain strips perpendicular to the fold, then cut smaller pieces from those strips (the first and second cuts in the cutting charts). It is a good idea to use one crosswise edge of your fabric to cut strips and to cut odd-size pieces from the opposite edge.

FABRIC REQUIREMENTS

Listed below are the basics—the big pieces you may have to buy. Consult the cutting charts for each block and cut the rest of the quilt from scraps in your fabric collection.

General Fabric Requirements

3¼ to 3½ yds. for background
¾ yd. for walkways
1½ yds. for sky
½ yd. for inner border
4 yds. for backing
74" x 74" piece of batting
⅝ yd. for binding

Choose interesting fabrics with lines, textures, stripes, and even whimsical designs. If you choose to use directional fabrics to simulate building materials, waves, etc., you may need to pay special attention when cutting.

Knowing the orientation of a piece will allow you to decide in advance whether you need to cut it along the crosswise or lengthwise grain. *Remember that cutting a tall building shape on the lengthwise grain may mean you need extra fabric.*

Working with dimensional prints can be tricky, but they really make this project come to life. The photographs that begin on page 25 show how students have used directional prints to create interesting effects.

Refer to the list below for an idea of how much fabric you will need for some of the smaller parts of the quilt:

Miscellaneous Fabrics

¼ to ½ yd. for houses and roofs
¼ to ½ yd. for lake
¼ yd. each of assorted fabrics for trees
⅛ yd. for tree trunks (more if it would make a good roof or siding)
⅛ yd. for flower bed
¼ yd. for windows
⅛ yd. for chimneys
⅛ yd. for doors

The Pieced Border

Before you begin to cut and piece the quilt, cut one 2" strip from the width of each fabric. Set the strips aside for the pieced outer border.

Embellishments

Add exciting details to your houses using machine or hand stitching. You can also use a Pigma permanent-ink fabric marker. Look at buildings in your surroundings for ideas and watch for tips in the block instructions about features to add and ways to use your sewing machine to create architectural details.

TOOLS

You will need the basic sewing supplies listed below:

Good fabric scissors
Pins
Seam ripper
Rotary cutter
6" x 24" acrylic quilter's ruler
Cutting mat
BiRangle™* (optional)
Tape measure
Sewing machine with neutral-colored cotton thread
Fabric-marking pen or pencil
Optional: 15"-square ruler

Available from That Patchwork Place.

GETTING ORGANIZED

1. Select as many fabrics as possible from your collection.
2. Before you shop for additional fabric, take the time to cut small swatches from each of the fabrics you plan to use. Glue samples of your fabrics on a 3" x 5" card to carry with you.
3. Take the 2"-wide strips you have cut from the width of each fabric for the pieced border. Put the border strips in a labeled plastic bag.
4. Keep your collection of fabrics for this project in a box or basket so that it does not get mixed in with your other fabrics.
5. If you have purchased the fabrics for the inner border, binding, and backing, label and set them aside.

Now you are ready to begin. One final note: As you cut, stick a small Post-it™ to each piece with the dimensions of the piece written on it. This will make the many small pieces easy to identify as you sew.

Cape Cod Cottage

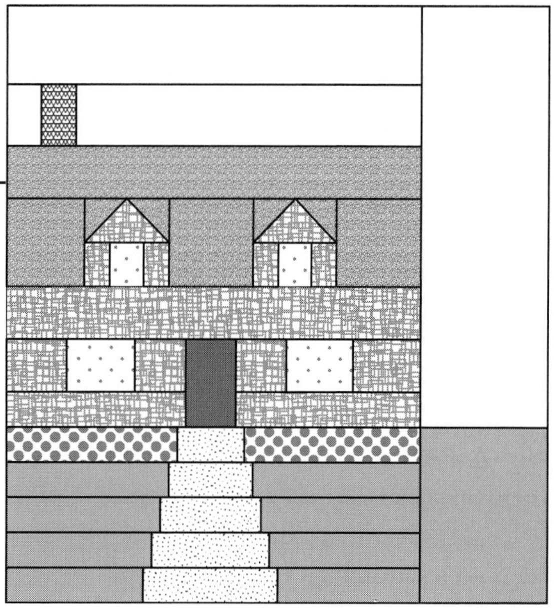

FABRICS: *background, walkway, sky, chimney, roof, siding, window, door, and flower bed. See pages 5–6 for yardage requirements.*

Cutting

FABRIC	FIRST CUT		SECOND CUT	
	NO. OF STRIPS	DIMENSIONS	NO. OF PIECES	DIMENSIONS
Background	1	1½" x 42"	2	1½" x 5¼"
			2	1½" x 5"
			2	1½" x 4¾"
			2	1½" x 4½"
	1	5½" x 5½"		
Walkway	1	1½" x 20"	1	1½" x 2½"
			1	1½" x 3"
			1	1½" x 3½"
			1	1½" x 4"
			1	1½" x 4½"
Sky	1	3" x 42"	1	3" x 12½"
			1	1½" x 2"
			1	2" x 10½"
	1	5½" x 13"		
Chimney	1	1½" x 2"		
Roof	1	3" x 42"	2	3" x 3"
			1	3" x 3½"
			1	2" x 12½"
			4	1½" x 1½"
Siding	1	2" x 42"	1	2" x 12½"
			2	2" x 2¼"
			2	2" x 2"
			2	1½" x 5¾"
			4	1" x 2"
			2	1½" x 2½"
Window	1	2" x 10"	2	1½" x 2"
			2	2" x 2½"
Door	1	2" x 3"		
Flower Bed	1	1½" x 12"	2	1½" x 5½"

Block Assembly

DORMER WINDOWS

1. Draw a diagonal line on the wrong side of each of the four 1½" roof squares. Place a roof square on 1 of the 1½" x 2½" siding pieces, right sides together. Stitch on the diagonal line. Trim the remainder of the *roof square only*, leaving a ¼"-wide seam allowance.

Repeat with another 1½" roof square on the other end of the rectangle. Make the second dormer in the same manner.

2. Sew a 1" x 2" siding piece to each side of a 1½" x 2" window. Add a dormer to the top of this unit. Repeat.

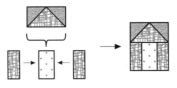

FIRST FLOOR WINDOW UNITS

Note: Before joining the windows to the siding pieces, you may want to sew through the center of the window pieces using a satin stitch to give the look of mullion bars. Stabilize the fabric with paper or interfacing as you stitch.

To construct the 2 window units, sew a 2" x 2¼" siding piece to the outer edges of each 2" x 2½" window. Sew a 2" siding square to the inner edge of each window. Now attach a 1½" x 5¾" siding piece to the bottom of each window unit.

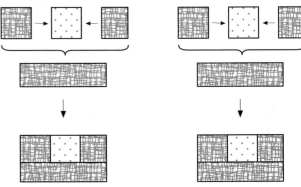

Finishing

1. Sew the illustrated units together into horizontal sections.

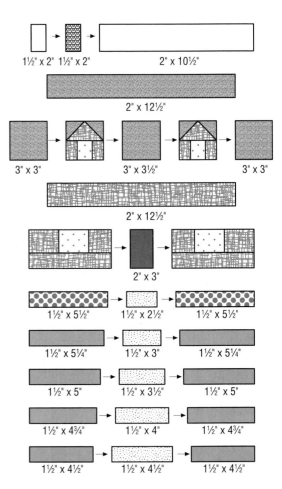

2. Sew the horizontal sections together to form the block.

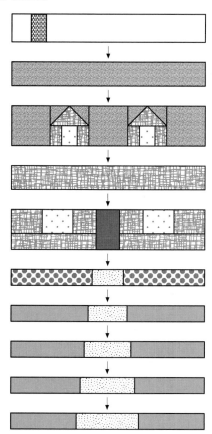

3. Sew the 3" x 12½" sky piece to the top of the block.

4. Sew the 5½" x 13" sky piece to the 5½" background square. Sew this section to the right side of the cottage, matching the sky/background seam to the flower bed/first floor seam.

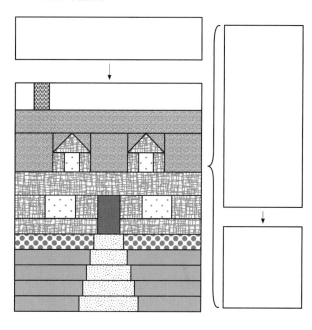

TRIMMING

To allow for variation in seam allowances, a cutting cushion has been added to the top and the right side of the block. The block should measure 16¼" wide and 17" long. If your seams were a perfect ¼" wide, the block will be larger than this. Trim the block to these dimensions, remembering to trim from the top and right only.

$\mathcal{F}$ARMHOUSE

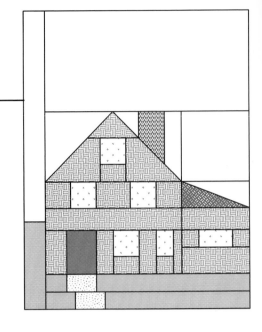

Farmhouses come in all shapes and sizes. They often have windows of different sizes and rooms added on. Many midwestern quilters have lived in old farmhouses like this one.

FABRICS: *background, walkway, sky, chimney, roof, siding, window, and door. See pages 5–6 for yardage requirements.*

Cutting

FABRIC	FIRST CUT		SECOND CUT	
	NO. OF STRIPS	DIMENSIONS	NO. OF PIECES	DIMENSIONS
Background	1	1½" x 24"	1	1½" x 1¾"
			1	1½" x 2¼"
			1	1½" x 9½"
			1	1½" x 9"
	1	2½" x 5½"		
Walkway	1	1½" x 5"	2	1½" x 2¼"
Sky	1	4½" x 15"	2	4½" x 4½"
			2	2" x 4½"
	1	2½" x 18"	1	2½" x 13"
			1	2" x 4½"
	1	7" x 12½"		
Chimney	1	1½" x 4½"		
Roof	1	2" x 4½"		
Siding	1	3" x 42"	2	3" x 3¾"
			2	1½" x 3"
			1	1¾" x 3"
			1	1" x 3"
	Trim remainder of strip to 2".		2	2" x 2"
			1	2" x 8½"
			1	2" x 2½"
			1	2" x 4½"
	1	1½" x 42"	2	1½" x 2"
			3	1½" x 1½"
			1	1½" x 8½"
			1	1½" x 4½"
Window	1	2" x 14"	4	2" x 2"
			1	1½" x 2"
			1	1½" x 2½"
Door	1	2¼" x 3"		

Block Assembly

ATTIC

1. Sew a 2" x 4½" sky piece to each side of the 1½" x 4½" chimney piece.

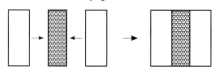

2. To construct the attic section, sew a 1½" x 2" siding piece to the bottom of a 2"-square window. Sew a 3" x 3¾" siding piece to each side of the window section. Sew the 2" x 8½" siding piece to the top of the window section.

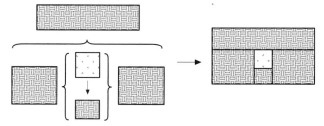

3. Draw a diagonal line on the wrong side of one 4½" square of sky fabric.

4. Position the 4½" square of sky fabric on the left side of the window section, right sides together, so that the diagonal line runs from the lower left corner to the upper right corner of the block.

5. Stitch on the line. Trim the *sky square only* to a ¼"-wide seam allowance. Press.

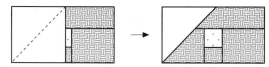

6. Draw a diagonal line on the wrong side of the sky/chimney section from the lower left to the upper right. Turn the sky/chimney section counterclockwise 90° so that the chimney runs horizontally. Position it on the right side of the window section with right sides together.

7. Stitch on the line. Trim the *chimney square only* to a ¼"-wide seam allowance. Press.

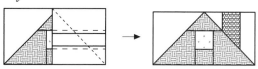

8. Sew the remaining 1½" x 2" siding piece to the bottom of the second 2"-square window. Sew a 1½"-square siding piece to the bottom of the 1½" x 2" window.

HOUSE ADDITION

1. Assemble the addition by sewing a 1½" siding square to each side of the 1½" x 2½" window.

2. Sew the 2" x 4½" siding piece to the bottom of the window section. Sew the 1½" x 4½" siding piece to the top.

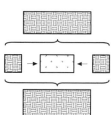

3. To construct the roof for the addition, place the 2" x 4½" sky rectangle and the 2" x 4½" roof rectangle wrong sides up on your work surface. Measure ¼" in from opposite corners and mark a diagonal line as shown.

4. Layer the 2 rectangles right sides together, matching lines, not edges.

5. Stitch along the line, sewing past the marks all the way out to the edges. Open, press, and trim the seam allowances to ¼".

6. Sew the roof to the top of the house addition.

Finishing

1. Sew the illustrated units into horizontal sections.

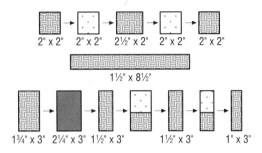

2. Sew the illustrated sections together.

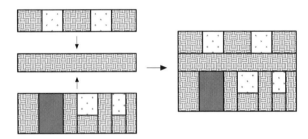

3. Sew a 4½" sky square to the right side of the roof section. Sew the addition to the right side of the first and second floor unit.

4. Sew the walkway together as shown.

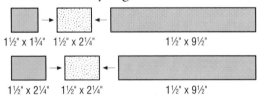

5. Sew the roof and house sections together. Sew the walkway to the bottom of the farmhouse.

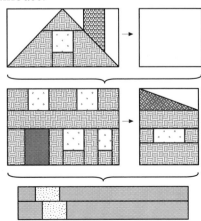

6. Sew the 7" x 12½" sky piece to the top of the house.

7. Sew the 2½" x 5½" background piece to the 2½" x 13" sky piece. Attach this section to the left side of the farmhouse, matching the lower edges.

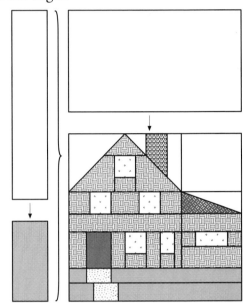

TRIMMING

The cutting cushion is on the top and left sides of the block. The block should measure 13¾" wide and 17" long. Remember to trim from the left and top only.

Embellishments

You might enjoy embroidering some flowers in front of this house. For the door, a French knot will give the look of a doorknob. Look at the quilt photographs on pages 25–32 for ideas.

$\mathscr{B}$ARN

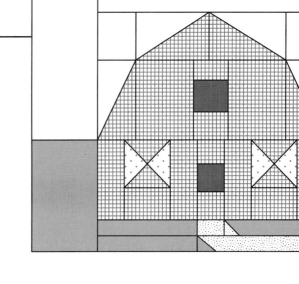

Examine the photos on pages 25–32. Notice that cutting the window or door squares from siding fabric makes the window or door appear to be closed. Using a different fabric for these squares creates the illusion that the window or door is open.

Imaginative use of fabric will enhance this block, as will chickens in the windows, hay in the loft, or even a billboard on the side of the barn.

FABRICS: *background, walkway, sky, siding, window, and door. See pages 5–6 for yardage requirements.*

Cutting

FABRIC	FIRST CUT		SECOND CUT	
	NO. OF STRIPS	DIMENSIONS	NO. OF PIECES	DIMENSIONS
Background	1	1½" x 42"	3	1½" x 7"
			1	1½" x 1½"
	1	5½" x 7½"		
Walkway	1	1½" x 15"	1	1½" x 2½"
			1	1½" x 9"
			1	1½" x 1½"
Sky	1	3" x 8"	2	3" x 3"
	1	5½" x 42"	1	5½" x 15½"
			1	5½" x 13"
	1	10" x 42"*		
Siding	1	4" x 42"	2	4" x 5½"
			2	2½" x 3½"
			2	1½" x 3½"
	1	2½" x 42"	2	2½" x 5½"
			1	1½" x 2½"
			2	2" x 5½"
	1	10" x 42"*		
Window	1	3½" x 3½"**		
	2	4¼" x 4¼"**		
Upper door	1	2½" x 2½"**		
Lower door	1	2½" x 2½"		
*Use this piece to cut bias rectangles. See directions below.				
**Cut this piece from siding or other fabric to achieve the desired effect.				

Cutting Bias Rectangles

1. Lay the 10" x 42" strip of sky fabric on your cutting surface with the right side down and the selvages to your right and left. Lay the 10" x 42" strip of siding fabric on the sky fabric, also right side down. Fold both fabrics in half by bringing the left-hand selvages over to meet the selvages on the right. The fold will be on the left. If the upper edge is not straight, trim the edge perpendicular to the fold.

Place fold on left

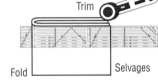

2. Place the BiRangle on the upper edge of the fabric. Place the 24" ruler on top of the BiRangle with one long edge along the diagonal line. Move this combination of BiRangle and long ruler along the top edge of the fabric until the ruler points directly at, or intersects, the lower right corner of the fabric. This creates a diagonal line across the fabric. Slide the BiRangle out of the way and cut along the diagonal on the right side of the ruler.

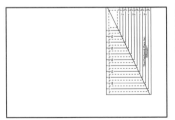

Place BiRangle™ with diagonal line pointing toward lower right hand corner

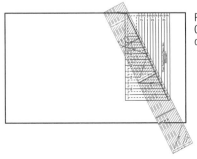

Place Cutting Guide on diagonal line

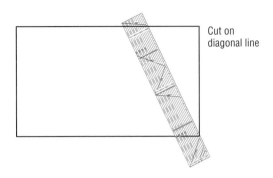

Cut on diagonal line

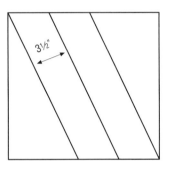

3. Make another cut 3½" away from and parallel to the first cut.

4. Separate the pairs of strips into 2 sets: those with the right side facing up and those with the right side facing down. Sew each set together with a ¼"-wide seam.

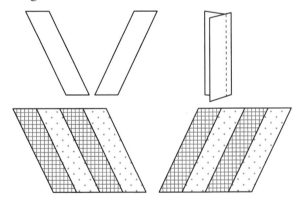

5. To cut rectangles, position the BiRangle so that the diagonal line is aligned with the seam. Make sure that the grain lines of the fabrics are parallel to the straight edge of the BiRangle. Use the BiRangle to cut the first 2 sides of the rectangle. Rotate the BiRangle 180°. Align the BiRangle's diagonal line with the seam line, and align the 3" line and the 5½" lines with the previously cut

edges of the fabric. Cut along the remaining 2 sides to form a 3" x 5½" rectangle.

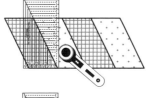
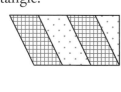

Cut 2 rectangles from each set of strips.

Block Assembly

WINDOWS, DOOR, AND WALKWAY

1. Place the two 4½" window squares right sides together. Draw a diagonal line on the wrong side of 1 square. Stitch ¼" away from the line on either side. Cut on the drawn line. Press the blocks open with the seam allowances to one side.

2. Place the blocks right sides together again with the seam allowances lying in opposite directions and seam lines matching. Draw a diagonal line from corner to corner on the wrong side of the top block, perpendicular to the first seam. Stitch ¼" away from the line on either side as in step 1. Cut on the drawn line.

You will get 2 blocks that look like this:

3. Press the window blocks. If necessary, trim them to 3½", making sure to trim from all 4 sides. Sew a 2½" x 3½" siding piece to the bottom of each window.

4. To make the door, sew the 2½"-square upper door to the 2½"-square lower door. Sew the 1½" x 2½" siding piece to the top of the door.

5. For the second-floor window, sew one 1½" x 3½" siding piece to the top of the 3½"-square window and another to the bottom of the window.

6. To create the walkway, draw diagonal lines on the wrong side of the 1½" walkway square and the 1½" background square. Lay the walkway square on the end of a 1½" x 7" background strip so that the diagonal line slants as shown. Stitch on the line. Lay the background square on the end of the 1½" x 9" walkway strip so that the diagonal line slants as shown. Stitch on the line.

Finishing

1. Sew the illustrated units together into horizontal sections.

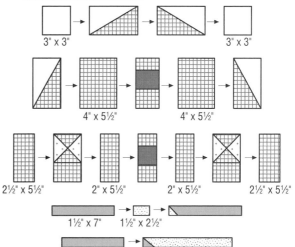

2. Join the horizontal sections.

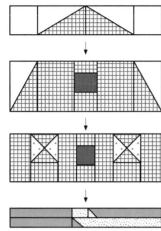

3. Sew the 5½" x 15½" sky piece to the top of the barn.
4. Sew the 5½" x 13" sky piece to the 5½" x 7½" background piece.
5. Attach this unit to the left side of the barn, matching lower edges.

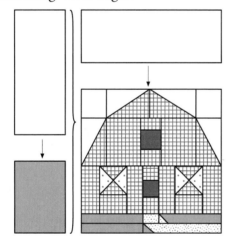

TRIMMING

The cutting cushion is on the top and left sides of this block. Trim the block to measure 19¼" wide and 19" long.

Embellishments

A weathervane would be a wonderful addition to the top of the barn. Make a vertical satin stitch line with an X across it. Add the letters *N*, *S*, *E*, and *W* to the ends of the X.

You can use reverse appliqué to add an appropriate animal to the weathervane at the top of the barn. Many fabrics on the market have animals that would work well. See the photographs on pages 25–32 for weathervane ideas.

REVERSE APPLIQUÉ

1. Place the animal fabric right side down on the wrong side of your barn, centering it above the peak.
2. Lower your feed dog, attach a darning foot, and free-motion stitch around the shape of the animal.
3. On the front, cut away the sky fabric inside your stitching to expose the animal.
4. Satin stitch around the animal with matching thread.

Apple Tree and Clothesline

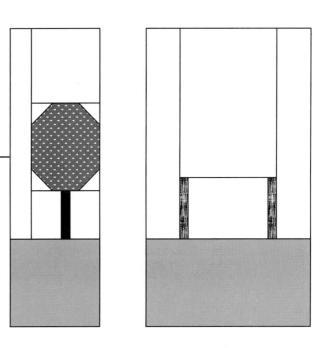

Finish the top section of your quilt by adding the apple tree and clothesline. Then join the blocks you have already made.

FABRICS: *background, walkway, sky, treetop, tree trunk, and clothesline pole. See pages 5–6 for yardage requirements.*

Cutting

FABRIC	FIRST CUT No. of Strips	FIRST CUT Dimensions	SECOND CUT No. of Pieces	SECOND CUT Dimensions
Background	1	5½" x 42"	1	5½" x 6¾"
			1	5½" x 11¼"
Walkway	2	2½" x 25"		
Sky	1	6¼" x 42"	1	6¼" x 9½"
			1	4½" x 4¾"
			1	4" x 5¼"
			1	3½" x 13"
	1	2¾" x 42"	1	2¾" x 13"
			1	2½" x 13"
			2	2¼" x 3¾"
			4	1¾" x 1¾"
Treetop	1	4½" x 5½"		
Tree trunk	1	1" x 3¾"		
Clothesline				
Pole	1	1" x 9"	2	1" x 4"

Block Assembly

APPLE TREE

1. Draw a diagonal line on the wrong side of each of the 1¾" sky squares. Place a square on each corner of the 4½" x 5½" treetop piece as shown. Stitch on the lines. Trim the *sky pieces only,* leaving a ¼"-wide seam allowance.

2. Sew a 2¼" x 3¾" sky piece to each side of the 1" x 3¾" tree trunk.

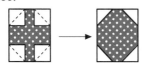

3. Sew the sky/tree trunk section to the bottom of the treetop piece. Sew the 4½" x 4¾" sky piece to the top of the tree.

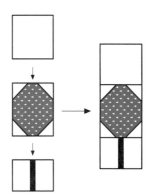

4. Attach the 2¾" x 13" sky piece to the left side of the tree. Sew the 5½" x 6¾" background piece to the bottom.

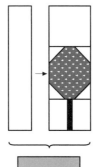

TRIMMING

The cutting cushion is on the top and left sides of this block. Trim to measure 5¾" wide and 17" long, cutting from the top and left sides only.

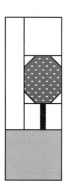

CLOTHESLINE

1. Sew a 1" x 4" clothesline-pole piece to each side of the 4" x 5¼" sky piece.

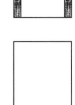

2. Sew the 6¼" x 9½" sky piece to the top of the clothesline.

3. Sew the 2½" x 13" sky piece to the right side of the clothesline; sew the 3½" x 13" sky piece to the left side of the clothesline.

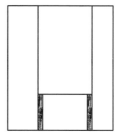

4. Sew the 5½" x 11¼" background piece to the bottom.

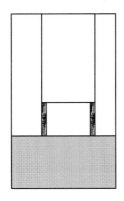

TRIMMING

The cutting cushion is on the top and left sides of this block. Trim to 10¼" wide and 17" long, cutting from the top and left sides only.

Embellishments

Add apples to the tree. String a clothesline between the poles and add clothes. There are several ways to do this. Wonderful buttons are available that look like clothes blowing in the wind, or you can create your own clothes.

1. Draw the shape of simple clothing on the wrong side of a scrap of fabric. Lay it on another piece of fabric, right sides together.
2. Stitch all the way around on the line of your clothing shape. Trim close to the stitching.
3. Cut through the center of one of the pieces, being careful not to cut through to the other fabric piece. Pull the fabric through the opening to turn the clothing piece inside out. (The clothing piece will be tacked against the quilt, so you will not see the hole.)
4. Stitch clothing to the clothesline and tack to the block.

ASSEMBLE THE TOP SECTION OF THE QUILT

1. Sew the Clothesline block to the left side of the Cape Cod Cottage block.
2. Sew the Farmhouse block to the left side of the Clothesline block.
3. Sew the Apple Tree block to the left side of the Farmhouse block.

This section should measure 44½" wide.

4. Sew the 2½" x 25" walkway strips together end to end. Cut to match the width of the section created in steps 1–3.
5. Sew walkway to bottom of section.
6. Sew the Barn block to the left side, lining up the bottom of the *building* with the top of the walkway. You have now completed the top section of the quilt.

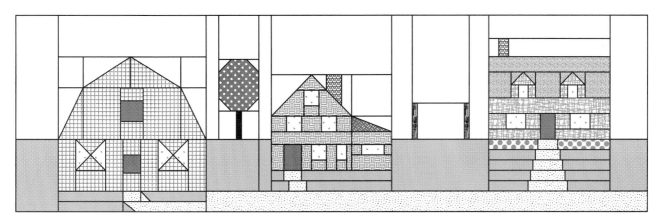

GROVE OF TREES

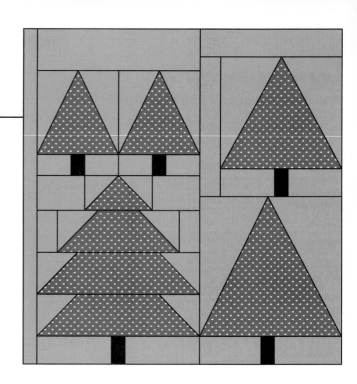

Create a grove of trees *and extra trees for use throughout the quilt.* Make sure your tree fabrics contrast well with your background fabric.

FABRICS: *background, trees, and tree trunk. See pages 5–6 for yardage requirements.*

Cutting

FABRIC	FIRST CUT		SECOND CUT	
	NO. OF STRIPS	DIMENSIONS	NO. OF PIECES	DIMENSIONS
Background	1	2" x 42"	2	1¼" x 2"
			10	2" x 2"
			1	2" x 13½"
	1	3¼" x 42"	2	3¼" x 9"
			1	3" x 6½"
			1	2½" x 5½"
			1	1½" x 5½"
	1	7" x 42"*		
Pine Tree	1	2" x 42"	1	2" x 3½"
			1	2" x 5"
			2	2" x 6½"
Other Tree	1	7" x 42"*		
Tree Trunk	1	1" x 9"		
*To be used with the BiRangle.				

Cutting Bias Rectangles

Create 5 triangular trees: 4 to complete the Grove of Trees and 1 to go next to the fence in the Signs and Fence block. If you like, you may make extra trees to add anywhere else in the quilt. Make triangular trees using the BiRangle method.

1. Lay the 7" x 42" green tree-fabric strip across the cutting surface with the right side down and the selvages to your right and left. Lay the 7" x 42" background strip on top, also right side down. Fold both fabrics in half by bringing the left-hand selvages over to meet the selvages on the right. Trim the edges perpendicular to the fold.

2. Place the BiRangle on the upper edge of the fabric. Place the 24" ruler on top of the BiRangle with one long edge along the diagonal line. Move this combination of BiRangle and long ruler along the top edge of the fabric until the ruler intersects the lower right corner of the fabric. This creates a diagonal line across the fabric. Slide the BiRangle out of the way and cut along the diagonal line (on the right-hand side of the ruler). Set aside the corner section you have just cut and use it in other piecing.

3. Make another cut 3½" away from and parallel to the first cut. Repeat 3 more times until you have 4 stacks of 4 strips each.

4. Separate the strips into 2 sets: those with right sides facing up and those with right sides facing down. There will be 8 strips in each set. Sew each set of strips together, using a ¼"-wide seam; alternate background and green fabrics as shown. Press the seams open.

5. To cut rectangles, position the BiRangle so that the diagonal line is aligned with the seam. Make sure the grain lines of the

fabrics are parallel to the straight edge of the BiRangle and the upper edge of the BiRangle is parallel to the upper edge of the strips.

Cut the following sizes from *each* set of strips to end up with either 2 or 4 mirror-image rectangles of each size:

For the Grove of Trees:
1 rectangle, 3" x 5½"
1 rectangle, 2½" x 4½"
2 rectangles, each 2" x 3½"

For the tree beside the fence:
1 rectangle, 2¾" x 5"

Block Assembly

PINE TREE

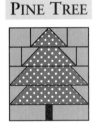

1. Set aside 2 of the 2" background squares. Draw a diagonal line on the wrong side of each of the remaining 8 background squares. Place a square on each corner of the 4 green pine-tree pieces as shown. Stitch on the line. Trim and press.

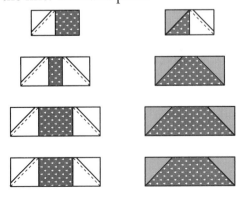

2. Sew the 2 remaining 2" background squares to each side of the top row.

3. Add a 1¼" x 2" back-
ground piece to each
side of the second row.

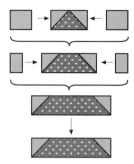

4. Sew all 4 rows together.
5. Sew a 3¼" x 9" background piece to each
side of the 1" x 9" tree-trunk piece. *This
section will provide all of your trunks.* Cut a
1¼"-wide strip off this section for the pine
tree. Sew to the bottom of the tree.

Block Assembly

1. Sew mirror-image bias
rectangles together to
create trees.

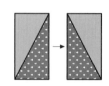

2. Add the tree-trunk sections. From the long
trunk piece set aside in step 5 of the Pine
Tree instructions above, cut 1¼"-long
trunks for the 2 small trees
and 1½"-long trunks for the
2 large trees. Center trunks
on the bases of the trees,
stitch, and trim excess background fabric from each side.

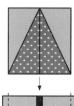

3. Assemble the left side of the block, adding
the 3" x 6½" background piece to the
top. Assemble the right side, adding the
1½" x 5½"
and
2½" x 5½"
background
pieces as
shown. Join
the 2 sides.

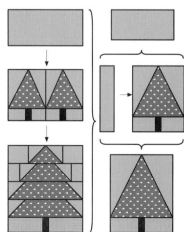

4. Sew the 2" x 13½" background piece to the
left side of the grove.

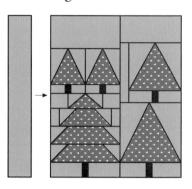

TRIMMING

The cutting cushion is on the top and
left sides of this block. Trim the block to
12" wide and 12½" long.

*Add a 1¼"-long trunk to the tree that will be
beside the fence. Save the tree for the Signs and
Fence block.*

AKE

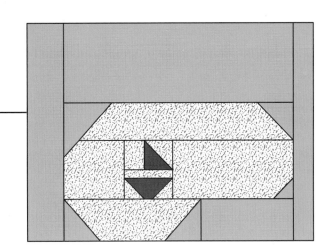

FABRICS: *background, lake, and sail and hull OR fishing shanty. See pages 5–6 for yardage requirements.*

Note: You will need ½ yard of lake fabric if the "waves" run parallel to the selvage (lengthwise). Otherwise, you will only need about ¼ yard.

Cutting

FABRIC	FIRST CUT		SECOND CUT		
	NO. OF STRIPS	DIMENSIONS	NO. OF PIECES	DIMENSIONS	
Background	1	5" x 42"	1	5" x 14¾"	✓
			1	3½" x 3½"	✓
	1	2½" x 42"	1	2½" x 6¼"	✓
			3	2½" x 2½"	✓
			1	2½" x 13"	✓
			1	1½" x 13"	✓
			1	1½" x 1½"	✓
Lake	1	3¾" x 42"	1	3¾" x 8"	
			1	3¾" x 4¼"	
			1	3" x 14¾"	
			1	2½" x 9"	
If you are adding a sailboat to your lake, cut the following:					
Lake	1	2½" x 42"	1	2½" x 2½"	
			1	1½" x 2½"	
			1	1" x 3½"	
			2	1¼" x 1¼"	
Sail	1	2½" x 2½"			
Hull	1	1¼" x 3½"			
		OR			
If you are adding a fishing shanty to your lake, cut the following:					
Lake	2	1¼" x 2¾"			
	2	1½" x 2"			
Shanty	2	1½" x 1½"			
	1	2" x 2¾"			

Block Assembly

SAILBOAT

1. Draw a diagonal line on the wrong side of the 2½" lake square. Place the 2½" sail square on the lake square, right sides together. Stitch on the line. Trim the *lake square only*, leaving a ¼"-wide seam allowance. Press.

2. Add the 1½" x 2½" lake piece to the left side of the sail square.

3. Add the 1" x 3½" lake piece to the bottom of the sail section.

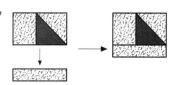

4. Lay the 1¼" lake squares on the 1¼" x 3½" hull piece with right sides together; draw diagonal lines as shown. Stitch on the lines. Trim the *lake squares only*, leaving a ¼"-wide seam allowance. Press. Sew to the bottom of the sail section.

FISHING SHANTY

If you do not want a sailboat on the lake, you can make this fishing shanty instead.

1. Draw a diagonal line on the wrong side of each of the two 1½" fishing-shanty squares. Lay each square on a 1½" x 2" lake piece, right sides together, with the diagonal line running from the upper corner to the middle of the lower edge as shown. Stitch on the line and trim the *shanty square only*, leaving a ¼"-wide seam allowance. Press.

2. Join the 2 pieces to create the roof.

3. Sew a 1¼" x 2¾" lake piece to each side of the 2" x 2¾" fishing shanty piece. Sew the roof to the top of this section.

Finishing

1. Draw a diagonal line on the wrong side of each of the following background squares: three 2½" squares, one 1½" square, and one 3½" square.

2. Place a 2½" background square on each end of the 2½" x 9" lake piece with right sides together as shown. Stitch on the line. Trim the *background squares only*, leaving a ¼"-wide seam allowance. Press.

3. Sew the 2½" x 6¼" background piece to the right side of the 2½" x 9" lake piece to complete the bottom section.

4. Sew the 3¾" x 4¼" lake piece to the left side of the sailboat or fishing shanty. Sew the 3¾" x 8" lake piece to the right side.

5. Lay the 1½" background square on the lower right corner of this section as shown. Stitch on the line and trim the *background square only*, leaving a ¼"-wide seam allowance. Press.

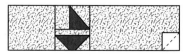

6. Stitch the bottom section to the sailboat/ fishing shanty section. Sew the 3" x 14¾" lake piece to the top.

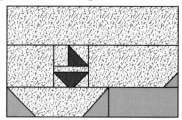

(continued on page 33)

PIECEFUL VILLAGE
*by Evelyn A. Zolotareff,
1992, Deerfield, Illinois,
68" x 63".
Buttons and appliqués embellish this summer scene.
Quilted by Fran Woodruff.*

*This barn is embellished with machine-embroidered
and appliquéd signs. The "barnyard" in front was
created by using a printed farm scene as the
background for the Fence block.*

ANOTHER TIME, ANOTHER PLACE
by Ellen Conoscenti,
1992–93, Yardley, Pennsylvania,
70" x 72".
Ellen used her parish church and the
A Touch of Amish quilt shop for inspiration.

Detail of barn with machine-embroidered
outlines and wind vane, plus pieced
barnyard animals from a Piecemaker
Keepsakes pattern by Naomi Norman.

OUR PIECEFUL VILLAGE
by Ginger FitzGibbon,
1993, Barrington, Illinois,
66" x 73".
Colorful clouds race across this village sky.

A machine-appliquéd
flower box and
hanging plants
decorate the gazebo.

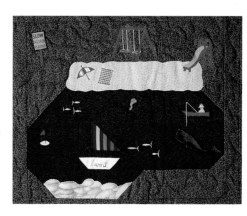

This lake has an embroidered
and appliquéd beach
playground, a fisherman,
whale, and fish.

**HELP ME,
I THINK
I'M FALLING**
*by Kathy Okon,
1992, Barrington,
Illinois,
66" x 70".
Bats fly across the
moon, ghosts
hang from the
clothesline, and
leaves litter
the ground in
this Halloween
quilt. Quilted
with help from
Carol Benson.
(The Halloween
figures come from
a Red Wagon
pattern by
Gerry Kimmel.)*

*Machine-appliquéd
trick-or-treaters
converge on this gazebo
hung with a seasonal
banner.*

*Machine-appliquéd fruits
and vegetables and a wind
vane adorn this barn.*

MY PIECEFUL VILLAGE
by Carol Gaza Benson, 1993, 63¾" x 67¼". Many Christmas Eve memories were pieced into this quilt. (The Santa was inspired by Piece on Earth by Radley House. Trees were inspired by Gerry Kimmel's Red Wagon designs.)

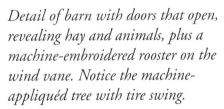

Detail of barn with doors that open, revealing hay and animals, plus a machine-embroidered rooster on the wind vane. Notice the machine-appliquéd tree with tire swing.

Santa flies over this farmhouse decorated with lace curtains and fancy, machine-embroidered door hinges.

BARRINGTON MEMORIES *by Sally Lynn Cran, 1993, Kennesaw, Georgia, 65" x 69". To commemorate her time in Barrington, Illinois, Sally Cran had the block-of-the-month patterns sent to her in Georgia.*

Appliquéd pigs wallow beside the barn as other animals peek out, and an Amish buggy stands nearby.

A machine-appliquéd freight train swings across the bottom of this quilt on an appliquéd track.

DEREK'S FIRST-GRADE QUILT
by Terry Atkinson, 1992-93, Elk River, Minnesota, 65¾" x 67". Terry used her child's school as the model for the playground in her quilt. Her sailboat is based on a pattern in Mary Hickey's Angle Antics.

Appliquéd flower beds, machine-embroidered lace curtains, and button flowers in the windows enhance this Cape Cod house.

Lace and rickrack transform the quilt-shop block into the quiltmaker's Victorian house with gingerbread trim.

MARY'S PIECEFUL VILLAGE
by Frances Kopp Krupka, 1992–93, Barrington Hills, Illinois. Frances adapted this scene and made it into a bed quilt for her daughter, Mary Margaret Krupka. For the upper tree border, she used a design that was published in the December 1992 edition of Quilter's Newsletter Magazine.

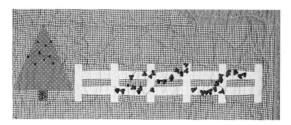

Embroidered ivy embellishes this Fence block.

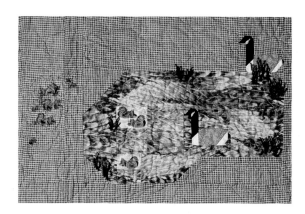

Duck print fabric and pieced Canada geese are used in this Lake block. Ducks are appliquéd into the embroidered grass, and embroidered cattails embellish the lake.

(continued from page 24)

7. With right sides together, lay the 3½" background square on the upper left-hand corner of the lake, and the remaining 2½" background square on the upper right corner. Stitch on the lines. Trim *background squares only*, leaving a ¼"-wide seam allowance. Press.

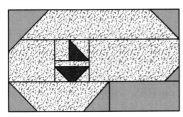

8. Sew the 5" x 14¾" background piece to the top.
9. Sew the 1½" x 13" background piece to the right side and the 2½" x 13" background piece to the left, stitching from the bottom up.

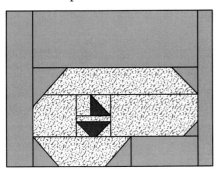

TRIMMING

The cutting cushion is on the top and left sides of this block. Trim the block to measure 17" wide and 12½" long.

Embellishments

You can have some fun adding details to your lake with machine or hand appliqué, embroidery, or other embellishment techniques. If the weather is warm, you can add waves at random across the lake. If you are lucky, there may be fish in your lake.

Of course, if there are fish, there will be fishermen and fishing poles. If the weather is cold and your lake is frozen, add a fishing hole by putting an oval or circle somewhere in the ice. See the photographs on pages 25–32 for more ideas.

$\mathscr{G}$AZEBO

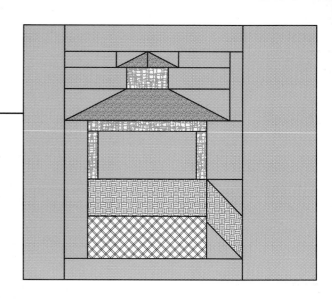

FABRICS: *background, roof, siding (2 or 3 different fabrics), and lattice. See pages 5–6 for yardage requirements.*

Cutting

FABRIC	FIRST CUT		SECOND CUT	
	NO. OF STRIPS	DIMENSIONS	NO. OF PIECES	DIMENSIONS
Background	2	2½" x 42½"		
	1	4½" x 42"	1	4½" x 13½"
			1	2½" x 13½"
			1	1½" x 9⅜"
	1	2¾" x 42"	1	2¾" x 5¼"
			1	2½" x 9⅜"
			2	2½" x 4½"
			1	2½" x 3¼"
			2	2½" x 2½"
	1	1⅝" x 42"	1	1⅝" x 7"
			2	1½" x 3½"
			2	1¼" x 3"
			2	1¼" x 2"
			1	1⅜" x 4"
Roof	2	1¼" x 2"		
	2	2½" x 4½"		
Siding #1	1	1½" x 2½"		
Siding #2	1	1" x 6¼"		
	2	1" x 2¾"		
Siding #3	1	2¼" x 6¼"		
	1	2½" x 4¼"		
Lattice	1	2½" x 6¼"		

Block Assembly

ROOF SECTIONS

1. For the upper roof, place the two 1¼" x 2" background pieces and the two 1¼" x 2" roof pieces wrong side up on your work surface. Measure in ¼" from opposite corners and mark as shown.
2. Draw a diagonal line on each piece, beginning and ending at the marks.

3. Layer the pieces right sides together so that the marks line up. Stitch along the line, sewing past the marks all the way out to the edges. Trim the *sky pieces only,* leaving a ¼"-wide seam allowance. Press.

4. Join the 2 roof sections.

5. Stitch a 1¼" x 3" background piece to each side of the roof to complete the upper roof section.

Repeat this technique to create the lower roof section, using the two 2½" x 4½" background pieces and the two 2½" x 4½" roof pieces.

SIDING #1

This section goes on top of the lower roof section, cutting off the peak.

1. Sew a 1½" x 3½" background piece to each side of the 1½" x 2½" siding piece as shown. Press seam allowances open.

2. Turn the siding section wrong side up. Make a mark on each seam, ¼" from the upper edge.

3. Lay this section on top of the lower roof section with right sides together. Slide the siding section down until the marks line up with the diagonal seams of the roof section. Pin. Join the 2 sections by stitching ¼" in from the edge of the siding section, through the marks.

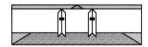

4. Trim the lower roof section even with the edge of the siding section.
5. Stitch the upper roof section to the top of the siding #1 section. Sew the 1⅜" x 4" background piece to the right side of the roof section, stitching from the bottom up.
6. Trim the background piece even with the top of the roof section.
7. Sew the 2½" x 9⅜" background piece to the top.

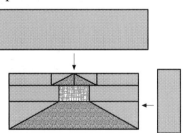

SIDING #2

Sew a 1" x 2¾" siding #2 piece to each side of the 2¾" x 5¼" background piece. Sew the 1" x 6¼" siding #2 piece to the top.

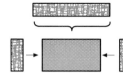

SIDING #3

Sew the 2¼" x 6¼" siding #3 piece to the bottom of the siding #2 section.

LATTICE

Sew the 2½" x 6¼" lattice piece to the bottom of the siding #3 piece.

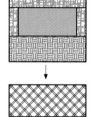

STAIRS

1. Draw a diagonal line on the wrong side of each of the two 2½" background squares. Lay the first square on the 2½" x 4¼" siding #3 piece with right sides together and the diagonal line running from upper left to middle right as shown. Stitch on the line. Trim the *background square only*, leaving a ¼"-wide seam allowance. Press.

2. Lay the second square on the siding #3 piece with right sides together as shown. Stitch on the line. Trim the *background square only*, leaving a ¼"-wide seam allowance. Press.

3. Sew the 2½" x 3¼" background piece to the top of the stair section.

4. Sew the stair section to the right side of the gazebo base.

5. Sew the 1⅝" x 7" background piece to the left side of the base.

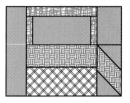

Finishing

1. Sew the roof section to the top of the gazebo base.
2. Sew the 1½" x 9⅜" background piece to the bottom of the gazebo.
3. Sew the 4½" x 13½" background piece to the right side of the gazebo. Sew the 2½" x 13½" background piece to the left side of the gazebo.

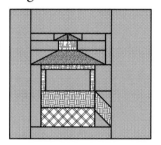

TRIMMING

The finished Gazebo block should measure 14½" wide and 12½" long. You may trim excess fabric from any side.

JOINING THE UNITS

Sew the Gazebo block, Lake block, and Grove of Trees block together as shown. Sew one 2½" x 42½" background strip to the top of the entire section and another to the bottom.

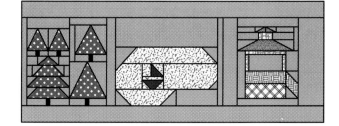

Quilt Shop

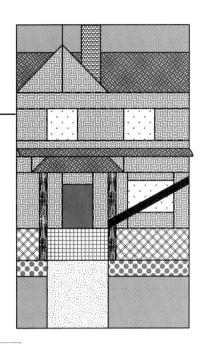

FABRICS: *background, walkway, chimney, roof, siding, window, door, stairs, post, lattice, flagpole, and flower bed. See pages 5–6 for yardage requirements.*

Cutting

FABRIC	FIRST CUT		SECOND CUT	
	NO. OF STRIPS	DIMENSIONS	NO. OF PIECES	DIMENSIONS
Background	1	5" x 42"	1	5" x 5½"
			1	2½" x 5"
			1	3¼" x 20½"
			1	2" x 3½"
			1	2" x 2"
			1	2" x 6"
Walkway	1	4½" x 6"		
Chimney	1	1½" x 4½"		
Roof	1	3" x 42"	1	3" x 3½"
			1	2" x 3"
			1	3" x 6"
			1	1½" x 6½"
			1	1¼" x 11½"
Siding	1	4" x 42"	4	1½" x 4"
			1	2" x 4"
			2	3½" x 3½"
			2	2½" x 2½"
			1	2½" x 3½"
	1	1½" x 42"	2	1½" x 11½"
			3	1½" x 1½"
			1	1½" x 4½"
			1	1½" x 3"
			1	1" x 3"
			1	1" x 2½"
Window	2	2½" x 2½"		
	1	2½" x 3"		
Door	1	2½" x 3½"		
Stairs	1	2½" x 4½"		
Post	2	1" x 6"		
Lattice	1	2" x 2½"		
	1	2½" x 5"		
Flagpole	1	1" x 8"		
Flower Bed	1	1½" x 2½"		
	1	1½" x 5½"		

Block Assembly

UPPER ROOF

1. To create the left side of the roof, sew the 2" x 3½" background piece to the 3" x 3½" roof piece.
2. To create the right side of the roof, sew the 2" background square to the 2" x 3" roof piece. Sew the 2" x 6" background piece to the 3" x 6" roof piece. Sew the 1½" x 4½" chimney piece between these 2 sections.

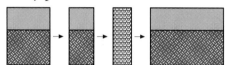

3. To make the roof peak, draw a diagonal line on the wrong side of each of the two 3½" siding squares. Place these 2 squares on the 2 roof sections as shown. Stitch on the lines and trim the *siding squares only,* leaving a ¼"-wide seam allowance. Press.

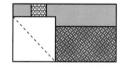

4. Sew the left and right sections together to complete the upper roof.

SECOND FLOOR

1. Sew a 2½" siding square to the outside edge of each of the 2½" window squares, and sew a 2½" x 3½" siding piece between them.
2. Sew a 1½" x 11½" siding piece to the top and bottom of the window section.

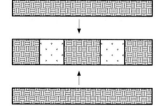

3. To create the porch roof, fold the 1¼" x 11½" roof piece in half with wrong sides together.

The piece should now measure ⅝" x 11½". Press. With raw edges aligned, baste to the bottom of the window section, using a scant ¼"-wide seam. Do not press seam open; the flap will be caught in the seam joining the window section to the first floor.

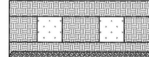
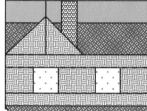

4. Sew the window section to the bottom of the upper roof section to complete the second floor.

FIRST FLOOR

1. Draw a diagonal line on the wrong side of each of two 1½" siding squares. Lay these squares on the ends of the 1½" x 6½" roof piece to create the roof over the door. Stitch on the lines. Trim the *siding squares only,* leaving a ¼"-wide seam allowance. Press.
2. Sew the remaining 1½" siding square to the left side and the 1½" x 4½" siding piece to the right side.

3. Attach this section to the bottom of the second floor. Press the porch-roof flap down toward the first floor.

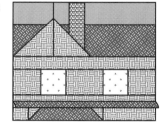

4. Sew the 2" x 4" siding piece to the 2" x 2½" lattice piece. Add a 1" x 6" post piece to the right side of this unit to create the left side of the first floor.

5. Sew the 1" x 2½" siding piece over the 2½" x 3½" door piece. Sew a 1½" x 4" siding piece to each side of the door. Sew the 2½" x 4½" stair piece to the bottom of the door to complete the door section.

6. Sew the left side of the first floor to the left side of the door section.

7. Sew the 1" x 3" siding piece to the top of the 2½" x 3" window piece. Sew the 1½" x 3" siding piece to the bottom of the window piece.

8. Sew a 1½" x 4" siding piece to each side of the window.

9. Sew the 2½" x 5" lattice piece to the bottom of this section. Attach the remaining 1" x 6" post piece to the left side to complete the window section.

FLAGPOLE

1. To add a flagpole, draw a line across the first-floor window section on the right side as shown. The exact angle of the flagpole is up to you. Cut on the line.

2. Sew the 1" x 8" flagpole piece between the 2 sections, making sure to line up the window as you sew the sections together. Trim the window section to 6" long, trimming from the top only.

Sew the window section to the right side of the door to complete the first floor. Join the first floor to the bottom of the second floor/lower roof section to complete the quilt-shop section.

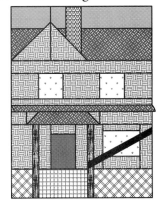

FLOWER BEDS AND WALKWAY

1. Sew the 1½" x 2½" flower-bed piece to the 2½" x 5" background piece for the left side of the front. Sew the 1½" x 5½" flower-bed piece to the 5" x 5½" background piece for the right side of the front.

2. Join the 2 sections to the 4½" x 6" walkway piece to complete the walkway section.

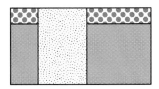

Sew the walkway to the bottom of the shop. Sew the 3¼" x 20½" background piece to the left side of the quilt shop.

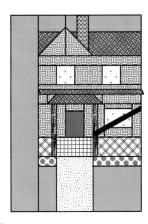

TRIMMING

The cutting cushion for this block is on the bottom and left sides. Trim so that the block measures 13¾" wide and 19½" long. Trim from the left side and the bottom only.

Embellishments

Make a small quilt, approximately 3" square, to tack onto your flagpole. You can piece a small quilt on paper or muslin using foundation piecing methods, or you can use a quilt-print fabric.

$\mathcal{S}$IGNS AND $\mathcal{F}$ENCE

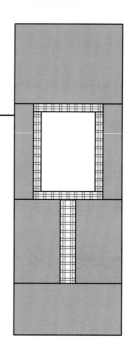
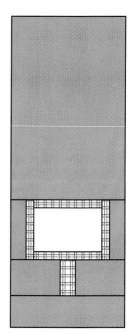

FABRICS: *background, signpost, sign background, sign frame, fencing, and extra tree (from Grove of Trees block instructions on pages 20–22). See pages 5–6 for yardage requirements.*

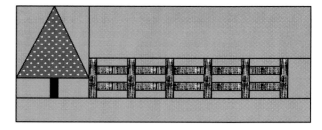

Light green

Cutting

FABRIC	FIRST CUT		SECOND CUT	
	NO. OF STRIPS	DIMENSIONS	NO. OF PIECES	DIMENSIONS
Background	1	13" x 42"	1	9½" x 13"
			1	2½" x 9½"
			1	5½" x 8"
			1	5" x 8"
			2	2¼" x 6"
			2	3¾" x 5½"
			2	2½" x 4½"
			2	2½" x 4"
	1	3¼" x 42"	1	3¼" x 15½" ✓
			1	3" x 20" ✎
			1	2½" x 3" ✓
	1	1" x 42"	3	1" x 13½" ✓
Signpost	1	1½" x 5½"		
	1	1½" x 2½"		
Sign Backgrounds				
Quilt Shop	1	3½" x 5"		
Church	1	3" x 4½"		
Sign Frames				
Quilt Shop	2	1" x 3½"		
Quilt Shop	2	1" x 6"		
Church	2	1" x 4½"		
Church	2	1" x 4"		
Fence	2	1 x 42"	2	1" x 13½" (rails)
			6	1" x 3" (posts)

Block Assembly

QUILT-SHOP SIGN

The background for the quilt-shop sign is 3½" x 5". If you choose to write on your sign, it is best to do this before you sew. Use either machine embroidery or Pigma permanent pens, which are great for writing directly on fabric.

1. Sew one 1" x 3½" sign-frame piece to the top of the sign; sew the other to the bottom of the sign.
2. Sew a 1" x 6" sign-frame piece to each side of the sign.
3. Sew a 2¼" x 6" background piece to each side of the framed sign.
4. Sew a 3¾" x 5½" background piece to each side of the 1½" x 5½" signpost piece.
5. Attach the post section to the bottom of the sign.
6. Sew the 5½" x 8" background piece to the bottom of the sign section; sew the 5" x 8" background piece to the top.

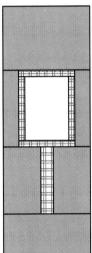

Trim the block to measure 7" wide and 19½" long, cutting from any side.

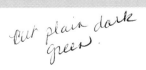
cut plain dark green.

CHURCH SIGN

Construct the church sign in exactly the same manner as the quilt-shop sign. Only the sizes of the pieces change. The background of the church sign measures 3" x 4½". Embellish before you piece.

1. Sew 1" x 4½" sign-frame pieces to the top and bottom of the sign piece. Sew a 1" x 4" piece to each side.
2. Sew a 2½" x 4" background piece to each side of the sign piece.
3. Sew a 2½" x 4½" background piece to each side of the 1½" x 2½" post piece. Join to the sign section.
4. Sew the 9½" x 13" background strip to the top. Sew the 2½" x 9½" background strip to the bottom.

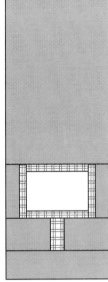

Trim the block from any side to measure 8¼" wide and 19½" long.

FENCE

1. Sew the three 1" x 13½" background pieces and the two 1" x 13½" fence pieces together to create the rails. Cut the rails into 5 segments, each 2½" wide.

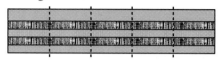

2. Sew the six 1" x 3" fence pieces to the rail segments as shown.

3. Sew the 2½" x 3" background piece to the right of the fence.
4. Sew the 3¼" x 15½" background piece to the top of the fence.
5. Sew the extra tree from the Grove of Trees block (pages 20–22) to the left of the fence.

6. Sew the 3" x 20" background piece to the bottom of the entire section, stitching from left to right (starting at the tree).

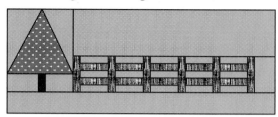

TRIMMING

The cutting cushion is on the bottom and right sides of this block. Trim the Fence/Tree section to 19¼" wide and 7¼" long, trimming from the bottom and right sides only.

$\mathcal{C}$HURCH

FABRICS: *background, walkway, roof, siding (1 or 2 different fabrics), window, and door. See pages 5–6 for yardage requirements.*

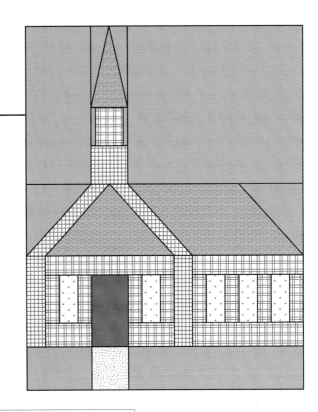

Cutting

FABRIC	FIRST CUT		SECOND CUT		
	NO. OF STRIPS	DIMENSIONS	NO. OF PIECES	DIMENSIONS	
Background	1	8½" x 42"	1	8½" x 10"	✓
			1	4" x 8½"	✓
			1	5" x 10"	✓
			1	4" x 5"	✓
			2	1½" x 4½"	✓
			2	¾" x 2½"	✓
			2	4" x 4"	✓
Walkway	1	2½" x 42½"			✓
	1	2½" x 37½"			✓
	1	2½" x 5"			✓
Roof	1	4" x 16"	1	4" x 10"	✓
			1	2½" x 4½"	✓
Siding #1	1	4" x 42"	1	4" x 7½"	✓
			8	1¼" x 3"	✓
			1	2" x 2½"	✓
	1	1½" x 42"	2	1½" x 6½"	✓
			2	1½" x 3"	✓
			1	1½" x 7½"	✓
Siding #2	1	1½" x 42"	2	1½" x 5"	✓
			2	1¼" x 7"	✓
	1	2½" x 2½"			✓
Window	1	1½" x 18"	5	1½" x 3"	✓
Door	1	2½" x 4"			✓

Block Assembly

SIDE OF CHURCH

1. Sew four 1¼" x 3" siding #1 pieces to three 1½" x 3" window pieces as shown.
2. Sew a 1½" x 6½" siding #1 piece to the top and bottom of the windows.

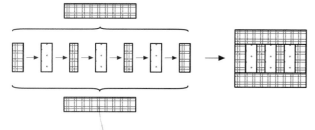

CHURCH FRONT

1. Sew a 1¼" x 3" siding #1 piece to each side of a 1½" x 3" window piece. Repeat with the remaining 2 siding pieces and 1 window piece.
2. Sew a 1½" x 3" siding #1 piece to the bottom of each section.
3. Sew the 2½" x 4" door between the 2 window sections. Attach the 1½" x 7½" siding #1 piece to the top of the entire window/door section.

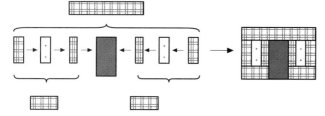

4. Sew a 1½" x 5" siding #2 piece to each side to complete the front section.
5. Sew the side of the church to the right side of the front section.

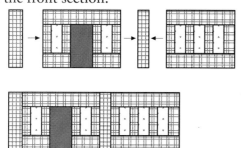

UPPER FRONT

1. Draw lines along all 4 sides of the 4" x 7½" siding #1 piece, ¼" in from the edges. Mark the center of the line along the upper 7½" edge. Draw a line from the lower left intersection of the edge lines (A) to the center of the upper edge line (B). Draw another line from the upper edge line (B) to the lower right intersection (C).
2. Trim ¼" beyond these diagonal lines.

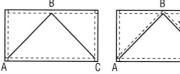

3. Sew a 1¼" x 7" siding #2 piece to each diagonal edge. Press; trim even with the upper and lower edges of the triangle.

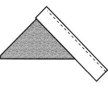

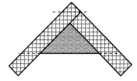

4. Draw a diagonal line on the wrong side of a 4" background square. Cut ¼" beyond that line. Sew the triangle to the left side of the background piece.

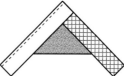

ROOF

1. Place the 4" x 10" roof piece right side down on your cutting surface. Measure 4" in from the lower right corner along the lower edge. Draw a line from that mark to the upper right corner. Trim ¼" outside the drawn line.

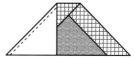

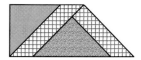

2. Turn the roof piece right side up. Lay a 4" background square on the right end of the roof section, right sides together. Draw a diagonal line as shown. Stitch on the line. Trim the *background square only,* leaving a ¼"-wide seam allowance. Press.

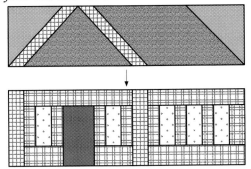

3. Sew to the right edge of the upper front to complete the church roof.
4. Join the roof and church front.

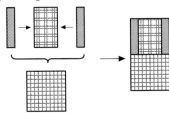

5. To create the tower, sew a ¾" x 2½" background piece to each side of the 2" x 2½" siding #1 piece. Sew to the top of the 2½" siding #2 square.

SPIRE

1. Draw a diagonal line on the wrong side of each of the two 1½" x 4½" background pieces as shown, starting and stopping ¼" in from the corners.
2. Draw lines on the wrong side of the 2½" x 4½" roof piece as shown. Start one line in the lower left corner, ¼" in from the corner, and end at the center of the top, ¼" down from the edge. Draw the other line from the

lower right corner in the same manner.

3. With right sides together, position a background rectangle on the roof rectangle so that one of the lines on the roof piece lines up with the line on the background piece. Stitch on the line. Press, trim, and repeat with the other background rectangle.

Finishing

1. Stitch the spire to the top of the tower.
2. Stitch the 8½" x 10" background piece to the right side of the tower and the 4" x 8½" background piece to the left side. Sew the unit to the top of the church.

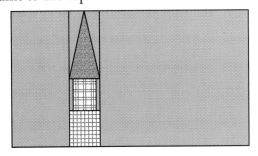

3. Sew the 5" x 10" background piece to the right side of the 2½" x 5" walkway piece. Sew the 4" x 5" background piece to the left side.

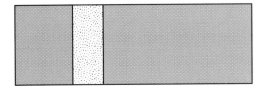

4. Sew this entire section to the bottom of the church, lining up the walkway with the door.

TRIMMING

The cutting cushion for this block is on the bottom. Trim the Church block to measure 19½" long, trimming from the bottom only.

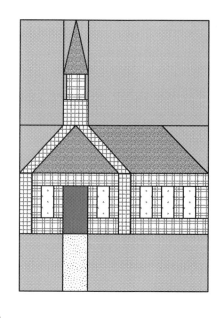

COMPLETE THE
QUILT SHOP/CHURCH SECTION

1. Sew the Church/Sign block to the left side of the Church block.
2. Sew the Quilt Shop block to the right side of the Church block.
3. Sew the Quilt Shop/Sign block to the right side of the Quilt Shop block.
4. Trim this entire section to 42½" wide, trimming from either end.
5. Sew the 2½" x 42½" walkway strip to the bottom of the section.
6. Sew this section to the bottom of the Gazebo/Lake/Trees section.
7. Sew the 2½" x 37½" walkway strip to the left side of the entire section.

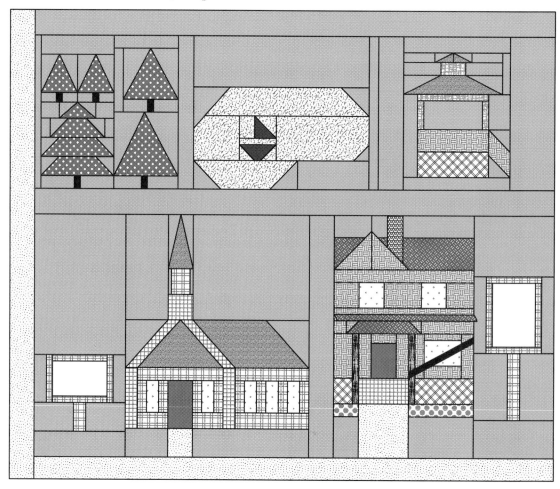

$\mathcal{L}$OG $\mathcal{C}$ABIN

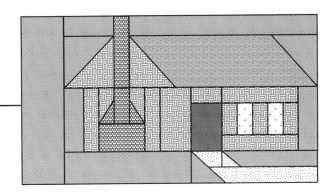

FABRICS: *background, walkway, chimney, roof, logs, window, and door. See pages 5–6 for yardage requirements.*

Cutting

light green

FABRIC	FIRST CUT		SECOND CUT		
	NO. OF STRIPS	DIMENSIONS	NO. OF PIECES	DIMENSIONS	
Background	1	3½" x 42"	1	3½" x 11"	✓
			2	3½" x 3½"	✓
		Trim strip to 2½" wide.	1	2½" x 8½"	
			1	2½" x 2½"	✓
	1	1½" x 42"	1	1½" x 12½"	✓
			1	1½" x 6½"	✓
			2	1½" x 4½"	✓
			1	1½" x 3½"	✓
Walkway	1	1½" x 15"	1	1½" x 8½"	✓
			1	1½" x 2½"	✓
			1	1½" x 1½"	✓
Chimney	1	1½" x 12"	1	1½" x 4½"	✓
			1	1½" x 2½"	✓
			2	1½" x 1½"	✓
	1	2½" x 3½"			✓
Roof	1	3½" x 12½"			✓
Logs	1	3½" x 14"	2	3½" x 3½"	✓
			1	2½" x 4½"	✓
	1	1½" x 42"	6	1½" x 2½"	✓
			2	1½" x 4½"	✓
			2	1½" x 5½"	✓
Window	2	1½" x 2½"			✓
Door	1	2½" x 3½"			✓

Block Assembly

ROOF

1. Draw diagonal lines on the wrong sides of one 3½" background square and one 3½" log square. Place the background square on the right end of the 3½" x 12½" roof piece, and the log square on the left end, right sides together. Stitch on the lines and trim the *background square only*, leaving a ¼"-wide seam allowance. Press.

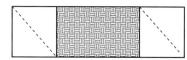

2. Sew the 1½" x 12½" background piece to the top of this section.

3. With right sides together, layer the remaining 3½" background square with the remaining 3½" log square. Draw a diagonal line on the wrong side of 1 square. Stitch on the line. Trim background square as before and press.

4. Sew the 1½" x 3½" background piece to the top of this section. Sew the 1½" x 4½" chimney piece between the 2 sections to complete the roof.

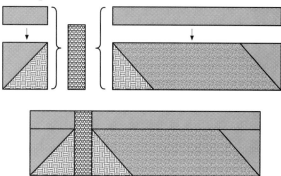

CABIN

1. Sew the two 1½" x 2½" window pieces between three 1½" x 2½" log pieces. Sew one 1½" x 5½" log piece to the top of the windows and another to the bottom as shown.

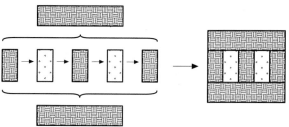

2. Sew a 1½" x 2½" log piece to the top of the door. Sew the door section to the left side of the window section. Sew the 2½" x 4½" log piece to the left side. Sew a 1½" x 4½" background piece to the right side to complete the front of the cabin.

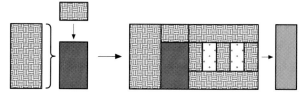

3. Draw a diagonal line on the wrong side of each of the two 1½" chimney squares. Lay each one on a 1½" x 2½" log piece, right sides together. Stitch on the line. Trim the *chimney squares only*, leaving a ¼"-wide seam allowance. Press.

4. Sew 1 of these units to each side of the 1½" x 2½" chimney piece.

5. Sew the 2½" x 3½" chimney piece to the bottom of this section. Attach a 1½" x 4½" log piece to each side. Add the remaining 1½" x 4½" background piece to the left side to complete the lower chimney section.

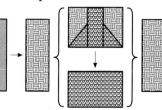

6. Sew the lower chimney section to the left side of the cabin front. Join the first floor and roof section, matching the chimney.

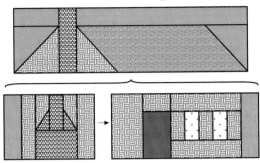

WALKWAY

1. Draw a diagonal line on the wrong side of the 1½" walkway square. Lay it on the left end of the 1½" x 6½" background piece, right sides together. Stitch on the line. Trim the *walkway square only*, leaving a ¼"-wide seam allowance. Press. Sew the 1½" x 2½" walkway piece to the left of this section.

2. Sew the 1½" x 8½" walkway piece to the bottom.

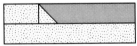

Draw a diagonal line on the wrong side of the 2½" background square. Lay it on the left side of the walkway section, right sides together. Stitch on the line. Trim the *background square only*, leaving a ¼"-wide seam allowance. Press.

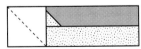

3. Sew the 2½" x 8½" background piece on the left side of the walkway section. Add the entire section to the bottom of the log cabin.

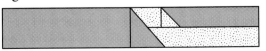

Sew the 4" x 11" background piece to the left side of the cabin. Trim even with the top and bottom edges of the cabin.

TRIMMING

The cutting cushion for this block is on the left side. Trim the block to 19¼" wide, trimming from the left side only. Sew the Tree/Fence section to the bottom of the Log Cabin block.

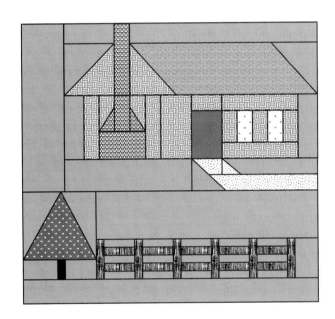

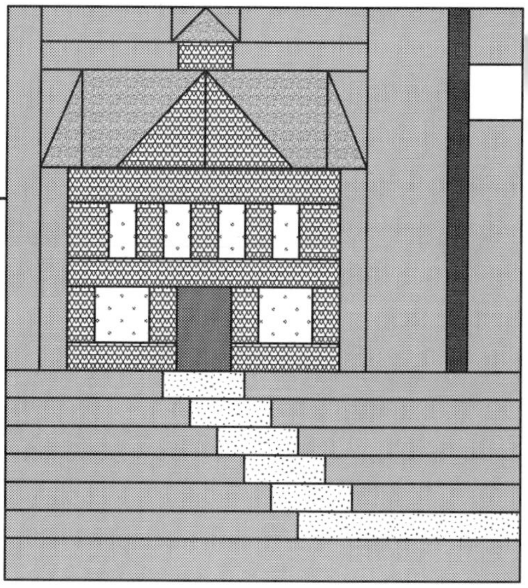

SCHOOL

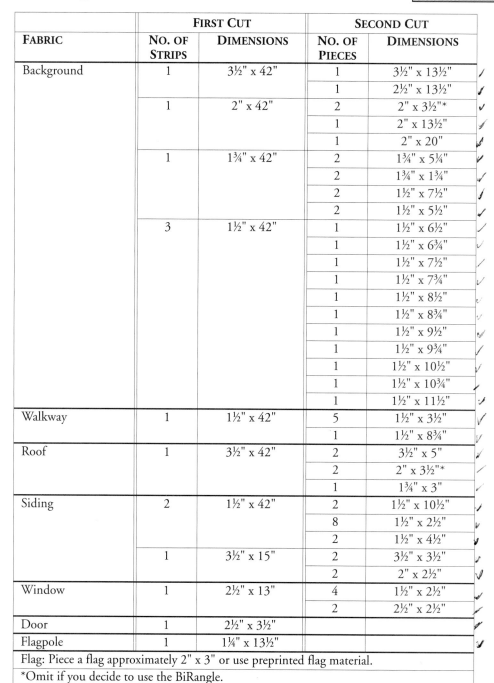

FABRICS: *background, walkway, roof, siding, window, door, flagpole, and flag. See pages 5–6 for yardage requirements.*

Cutting

light green

FABRIC	\- FIRST CUT \- NO. OF STRIPS	DIMENSIONS	\- SECOND CUT \- NO. OF PIECES	DIMENSIONS
Background	1	3½" x 42"	1	3½" x 13½"
			1	2½" x 13½"
	1	2" x 42"	2	2" x 3½"*
			1	2" x 13½"
			1	2" x 20"
	1	1¾" x 42"	2	1¾" x 5¼"
			2	1¾" x 1¾"
			2	1½" x 7½"
			2	1½" x 5½"
	3	1½" x 42"	1	1½" x 6½"
			1	1½" x 6¾"
			1	1½" x 7½"
			1	1½" x 7¾"
			1	1½" x 8½"
			1	1½" x 8¾"
			1	1½" x 9½"
			1	1½" x 9¾"
			1	1½" x 10½"
			1	1½" x 10¾"
			1	1½" x 11½"
Walkway	1	1½" x 42"	5	1½" x 3½"
			1	1½" x 8¾"
Roof	1	3½" x 42"	2	3½" x 5"
			2	2" x 3½"*
			1	1¾" x 3"
Siding	2	1½" x 42"	2	1½" x 10½"
			8	1½" x 2½"
			2	1½" x 4½"
	1	3½" x 15"	2	3½" x 3½"
			2	2" x 2½"
Window	1	2½" x 13"	4	1½" x 2½"
			2	2½" x 2½"
Door	1	2½" x 3½"		
Flagpole	1	1¼" x 13½"		

Flag: Piece a flag approximately 2" x 3" or use preprinted flag material.

*Omit if you decide to use the BiRangle.

Block Assembly

"Build" the school from the top down.

BELL TOWER

1. To make the peak of the tower, draw a diagonal line on the wrong side of each of the two 1¾" background squares. Lay 1 square on the 1¾" x 3" roof piece with right sides together. Stitch on the line. Trim and press open. Layer the second square as shown. Stitch on the line. Trim the *background square only,* leaving a ¼"-wide seam allowance. Press.
2. Sew a 1¾" x 5¼" background piece to each side.

3. Sew a 1½" x 5½" background piece to each side of one 1½" x 2½" siding piece. Join to the peak.

ROOF

1. Draw a diagonal line on the wrong side of each of the two 3½" siding squares. With right sides together, layer the two 3½" x 5" roof pieces as shown. Stitch on the line. Trim the *siding squares only,* leaving a ¼"-wide seam allowance. Press.
2. Join so that the siding pieces are in the center of the section.

You can create the outside edges of the roof section in one of two ways. The first is the BiRangle method (refer to page 14 for more information). If you use the BiRangle, you will need 2 mirror-image rectangles, each 2" x 3½".

You may also construct the outer edges in the following manner.

1. Place the two 2" x 3½" background pieces and the two 2" x 3½" roof pieces *wrong sides up* on your work surface. Measure in ¼" from each corner and mark as shown.

2. Layer a background piece and a roof piece right sides together so that the marks line up. Stitch along the line, sewing past the marks all the way out to the edges. Trim, press, and repeat with the other 2 pieces.

3. Sew the rectangles to the outside edges of the roof as shown.

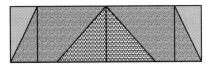

4. Sew the entire section to the bottom of the bell tower.

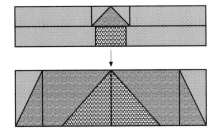

SECOND FLOOR

1. Sew the window and siding pieces together as shown. The outside siding pieces measure 2" x 2½". All of the other siding and window pieces measure 1½" x 2½".

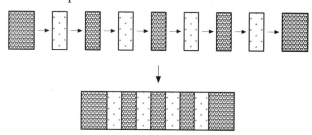

2. Sew a 1½" x 10½" siding piece to the top and bottom of the windows.

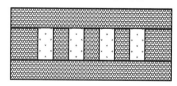

FIRST FLOOR

1. Sew a 1½" x 2½" siding piece to each side of both 2½"-square windows.
2. Sew a 1½" x 4½" siding piece to the bottom of each window.
3. Attach a window section to each side of the 2½" x 3½" door piece to complete the first floor.

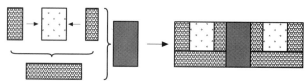

4. Join the first and second floors. Sew a 1½" x 7½" background piece to each side of the building.

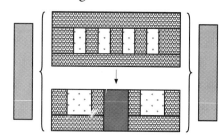

5. Sew the entire section to the bottom of the roof.

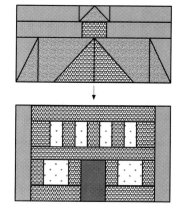

6. Make a pieced or printed flag, about 2" x 3" in size.

BACKGROUND AND FLAGPOLE

Sew from the top down.

1. Join the 2" x 13½" background piece to the left side of the school. Trim the background even with the bottom of the school.
2. Sew the 3½" x 13½" background piece to the left side of the 1¼" x 13½" flagpole piece. Sew the 2½" x 13½" background piece to the right side, catching the flag in the seam, approximately 1½" to 2" down from the top. Remember to place the front of the flag against the pole and then lay the background piece on both—and keep track of which way is up!

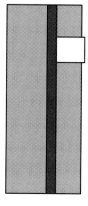

3. Join this section to the right side of the school. Trim the background/flagpole piece even with the bottom of the school.

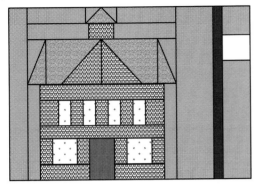

WALKWAY

To create the walkway, sew the following walkway and background pieces together into horizontal rows. Sew the rows together.

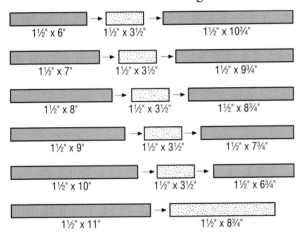

Sew the entire walkway section under the school. Sew a 2" x 20" background piece to the bottom.

TRIMMING

The cutting cushion for this block is on the left side. Trim to 19¼" wide, trimming from the left side only.

JOINING THE UNITS

1. Sew the School block to the bottom of the Log Cabin/Fence section. Trim the entire section to 37½" long, trimming from the bottom only.
2. Sew this section to the left side of the large Church/Quilt Shop/Lake section.
3. Attach this section to the bottom of the Barn/Farmhouse/Cape Cod section.
4. Take the two 4½" background strips you set aside when cutting fabric for the Cape Cod Cottage block. Sew them together to create 1 long strip. Measure the bottom edge of your quilt top. (If you have trimmed your blocks carefully, it should measure 63¼".) Cut your strip to the exact measurement of your quilt top. Sew the strip to the bottom of the quilt.

Congratulations, your village is finished!

FINISHING

Fabrics

2" x 42" strips, cut from fabrics used throughout the quilt, for pieced border
½ yd. for inner border and cornerstones
⅝ yd. for binding
4 yds. for backing
74" x 74" square of batting

Cutting

8 strips, each 1½" x 42", for inner border
4 squares, each 3" x 3", for cornerstones
8 strips, each 2¼" x 42", for binding

Inner Border

1. Sew two 1½" inner border strips together to form 1 long strip. Repeat with the remaining 6 strips for a total of 4 long strips.

2. Measure the length of your quilt in several places, measuring through the center of the quilt rather than along the edges.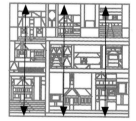
Take the average of those measurements and cut 2 of the long border strips to that exact, average measurement.

3. With right sides together, place the center of your strip at the center of the quilt side. Pin, starting with a pin at the center and one at each end, easing in fullness (if any) with additional pins. Stitch. Repeat with the other side. Press the seam allowances toward the border.

4. Add the top and bottom inner borders in the same manner.

Pieced Border

To make the pieced border, use the reserved 2"-wide strips you cut from each fabric. Sew those strips together into bands for your pieced outer border. You will need at least 16 (full-width) strips.

1. Sew the strips together, press. Cut into 3" segments.

2. Measure the length of the quilt including the inner border. Piece segments together until you have two strips slightly larger than the side inner border measurement. Trim to that exact measurement. Sew a pieced border to each side, easing as needed.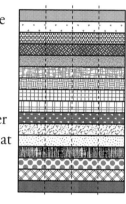

3. Measure the width of the quilt including inner borders and pieced side borders. Trim the pieced border strips to that measurement, trimming from both ends. Sew a 3" cornerstone to each end of the border strips. Sew the top and bottom pieced borders with cornerstones to the quilt top, lining up the cornerstones with the pieced borders on the sides as shown.

4. Trim the selvages from the 4-yard backing piece. Cut it into two 2-yd. pieces. Sew the pieces together along the selvage edges.

5. Layer the backing, batting, and quilt top. Baste or pin to secure the layers. Quilt as desired.

6. Sew the 8 binding strips together end to end. Press in half lengthwise, wrong sides together. Lay the binding strip on the front of the quilt and sew to edge of quilt, mitering the corners. Hand stitch the binding to the back of the quilt.

7. Sew buttons and other embellishments to the front if desired. Add a personal label to the wrong side of the quilt.

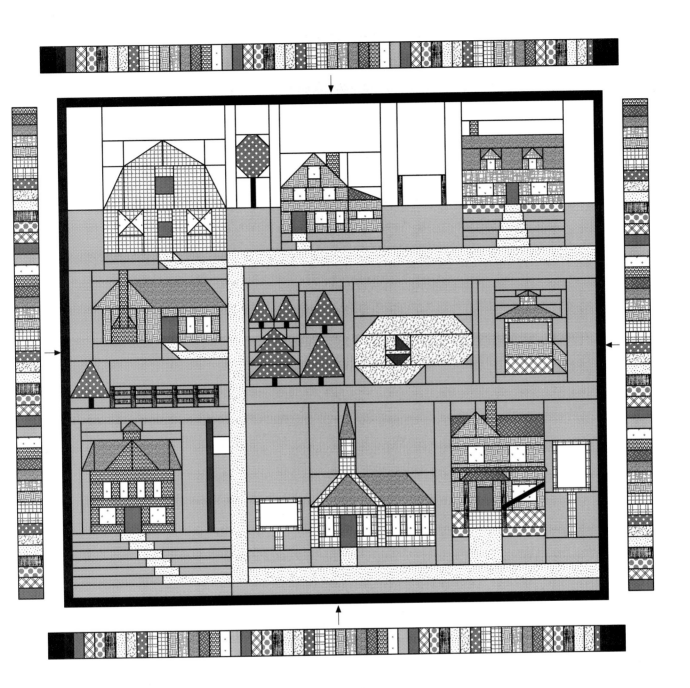

SOURCES FOR SUPPLIES

Porcelain Buttons
Cocanower Porcelain Art
21 Lamplight Lane
Edwardsville, IL 62025

Quilt Labels by Kim
A Touch of Amish, ltd.
126 Garfield Street
Barrington, IL 60010

MINIATURE CONVERSION CHART (IN INCHES)

REGULAR SIZE	MINIATURE SIZE	REGULAR SIZE	MINIATURE SIZE	REGULAR SIZE	MINIATURE SIZE
1	¾	6¼	3⅜	11½	6
1¼	⅞	6½	3½	11¾	6⅛
1½	1	6¾	3⅝	12	6¼
1¾	1⅛	7	3¾	12¼	6⅜
2	1¼	7¼	3⅞	12½	6½
2¼	1⅜	7½	4	12¾	6⅝
2½	1½	7¾	4⅛	13	6¾
2¾	1⅝	8	4¼	13¼	6⅞
3	1¾	8¼	4⅜	13½	7
3¼	1⅞	8½	4½	13¾	7⅛
3½	2	8¾	4⅝	14	7¼
3¾	2⅛	9	4¾	14 ¼	7⅜
4	2¼	9¼	4⅞	14½	7½
4¼	2⅜	9½	5	14¾	7⅝
4½	2½	9¾	5⅛	15	7¾
4¾	2⅝	10	5¼	15¼	7⅞
5	2¾	10¼	5⅜	15½	8
5¼	2⅞	10½	5½	15¾	8⅛
5½	3	10¾	5⅝	16	8¼
5¾	3⅛	11	5¾	16¼	8⅜
6	3¼	11¼	5⅞	16½	8½

MEET THE AUTHOR

Lynn Rice lives in Barrington, Illinois, with her husband, Art. They have three college-age children, Andrew, Sarah, and Daniel. The Rice household also includes a minimum of four dogs, more when there is a litter of schnauzer puppies.

Lynn began sewing as a child, but really became interested in quilts in the seventies. In 1986 she opened her own quilt shop, A Touch of Amish, ltd., when she found a source of Amish quilters. It seemed to be just the way to get her own tops hand quilted, and she knew other quilters would have the same need.

From a start with a few quilting supplies and a handful of bolts, the shop has grown to thousands of bolts, books, supplies, classes, sewing machines, and free demonstrations. The atmosphere of quilting enthusiasm and wonderful, helpful employees, with an occasional puppy underfoot, makes it a real haven for quilters.